WestBow Press books may be ordered through booksellers or by contacting:

WestBow Press
A Division of Thomas Nelson & Zondervan
1663 Liberty Drive
Bloomington, IN 47403
www.westbowpress.com
844-714-3454

Scripture quotations are taken from the Holy Bible, King James Version.

ISBN: 979-8-3850-0971-8 (sc)
ISBN: 979-8-3850-0972-5 (e)

Library of Congress Control Number: 2023919215

Print information available on the last page.

WestBow Press rev. date: 10/25/2023

WESTBOW
PRESS®
A DIVISION OF THOMAS NELSON
& ZONDERVAN

CONTENTS

PREFACE

During the many years I worked with people who had a life-threatening illness, were in crisis, or were experiencing the death of a loved one, the adults often voiced concern for their children. These Parents, grandparents, or caregivers asked how they could help their children or young person cope with the crisis or loss related to death. Some have asked how to tell young children that their loved one has died.

First, it is important for adults to understand the signs and symptoms of crisis or grief and loss themselves. The best way to help your child is to understand the child's age as it relates to developmental life stage. (You may refer to chapter 8 in this book to identify your child's developmental stage.) Clarify what your child understands about death.

It is also helpful to understand the "normal" reaction to crisis or loss, which is also identified in this book. Identify your own as well as your child's usual coping style in dealing with difficult things in life. For children who like to draw, perhaps using art and drawing would be ways to explore and express their feelings. This book will help your child *and* you to identify and learn effective coping strategies throughout the child's lifetime.

CHAPTER 1

Meet My Family

A merry heart doeth good like a medicine.
Proverbs 17:22 †

Let me introduce you to my family. My dad's name is Joe Senior. Of course, his middle name is not Senior, but that is what Mom calls him. To us, he is just Dad. Dad is kind of tall. He works hard all week. He takes mail to all the people in our neighborhood. Sometimes he tells us about funny things that happened on his mail route.

My mother's name is Mary. She can make people laugh. Dad says that Mom can make sad people happy just by making them laugh! Mom treats people like she cares about them, even if she does not know them very well.

Mom says laughter is like a feel-good medicine, and that is what the Bible says. Sometimes she just says "Proverbs 17:22," which says, "A merry heart doeth good like a medicine." All of us laugh when she says that because we know what Proverbs 17:22 means.

My brother's name is Joseph, but we call him Joe Junior. Joe Junior was two years old when I was born. He has dark brown hair. Joe is now eleven years old.

Joe is funny like Mom. He does not get mad. He is nice to everyone, even people who are mean to other people. I wish I could be like Joe!

Joe likes to read. His desk has a stack of books on it. He can read one book every day. Mom says that Joe started reading when he was four years old.

Joe likes me to walk to the library with him. It is three blocks from our house. I do not like to walk to the library with him, but I love being with him! Sometimes Joe helps me with my homework. He is so smart.

Molly Mae is my sister. She is five years old. I was four years old when Molly Mae was born. She had very dark hair when she was born. It looked a lot like Joe's hair color. When she was four months old, all her hair fell out. She didn't look very pretty when her hair came out. I cried because I thought something was wrong with her. Grandmama Mae said that Molly Mae's hair would grow back. She told me that almost everyone loses their hair when they are about four months old.

When Molly had new hair, it was a light reddish-blond. Mom calls it "strawberry blond." People say that she is pretty. I am just glad that she has hair again!

Molly Mae was named after our grandmothers. Grandmama Mary Mae Stuart is our mom's mother. Dad calls her Mary. Grandpa James Antony Stuart is my mom's father. Some people call him Jim. Grandpa and Grandmama live about five miles from us. They live on three acres and have some animals. They have two dogs, one momma cat, and four baby kittens.

Butters, the momma cat, runs very fast. She seems to slip out of my hands when I hold her, and that is how she got her name. She is so slippery! Butters catches mice. They are kind of cute, until they are dead and Butters leaves them at the back porch. Granddad gives her a treat after she catches a mouse—he says that is her reward. He says when Butters leaves dead mice at the back door, she is rewarding him, and Butters thinks the dead mouse is a gift to them.

Dad's father's name is Granddad Joseph George Walter. People call him George. Grams Molly Jane Walter is Dad's mother. Other people call her Jane. Granddad and Grams Walter live two blocks from us. Their house is the big white one with a white picket fence. In the front yard is a big oak tree with a swing that we love to swing in. In fact, we all love to spend time with Granddad and Grams.

Sometimes Mom walks over to their house so that she can swing too. She says that it helps her to think and pray, even if she just sits in the swing. Mom loves to quote the scripture, "For ye shall go out with joy and be led forth with peace: the mountains and the hills shall break forth before you into singing, all the trees of the fields shall *clap* their hands" (Isaiah 55:12). Sometimes I hear Mom singing or humming. Mom says that she loves trees. I think she loves the Bible more!

Oh, I forgot to tell you about me! My name is Antony James. I like to be called Tony. I am nine years old and am in the fourth grade. My teacher's name is Mrs. Bates.

I love to journal, write stories, and draw pictures. Mom, Dad, and my grandparents say that I am an artist. I do not think that I am very good. It does make me feel good, though, when they say that to me. I think it is like a feel-good medicine when people say nice things!

We have aunts, uncles, and lots of cousins. Maybe I will talk about them later.

CHAPTER 2

Our Dog, Ginger

And when the Lord saw her, he had compassion on her,
and said unto her, Weep not.
Luke 7:13

"Ginger, stop!"

Ginger, our dog, stopped chasing the ball. She started barking and running back and forth along the inside of the fence.

Mom hollered out the window, "Be careful, Tony, that Ginger doesn't get through the gate!"

When Ginger barked and ran, I could not catch her. It was as if she didn't even hear me. I yelled for Ginger to stop, but she did not stop.

"Mom!" I screamed when I heard tires squealing. We heard Ginger yelping loudly like she was hurt. It hurt my ears and made me cry because I just knew that she was hurt. Mom started to cry too.

The driver got out of his car and said, as he wiped away a tear, "I am so sorry. I didn't see your little dog."

Mom, who was still crying, said, "I think her left leg looks broken."

Dad drove up in his old red truck. Molly saw Ginger whimpering. Dad, Joe, and Molly got out of the truck. Molly was crying loudly. Mom told Molly that she should go in the house, but Dad said, "Molly should stay here with all of us. Then she will see how badly Ginger is hurt."

Molly asked what was wrong with Ginger. Joe had tears in his eyes.

Joe found a box, and Dad gently put Ginger in it. Mom, Joe, Molly, and I were crying.

I knew it was all my fault. We all got into Mom's blue van. Dad drove to the animal hospital.

Dr. Miller, the veterinarian, talked softly to Ginger. Ginger did not move much. He put a cast on her left leg. Ginger cried out every time Dr. Miller moved her leg. In fact, Ginger whimpered every time she was moved, even just a little bit.

Dr. Miller told Mom and Dad that the tire also hurt Ginger's insides. He said that she might be bleeding inside her tummy. Ginger did not seem like Ginger. She stopped wagging her tail. She did not want to get up and play. Ginger did not want to eat, not even her favorite treats.

Joe tried to pick up Ginger to hold her. Ginger looked up at Joe and cried softly. We all cried every time Ginger cried out.

The next day, Dad and Mom took Ginger back to Dr. Miller. We all went to the vet together. Dr. Miller told us that Ginger was bleeding inside her tummy.

Dr. Miller looked sad, just like Ginger was his own dog. He said she was dying. He said, "Ginger needs surgery." He explained that surgery would cost a lot of money and told Dad and Mom that Ginger would still die. "She is just too sick to live."

Molly started to weep. When Molly did that, it felt like she was weeping for all us. I knew it was my fault. I had let Ginger get out of the yard. Molly asked, "Is she going to die? Can we pray? Jesus has healed me before when we prayed. I know if we all prayed, Jesus would heal her!"

Molly made us all bow our heads and pray for Ginger. Mom said to Molly, "God does hear our prayers. God knows what is best, even for Ginger. He does answer our prayers, but sometimes He doesn't answer the way we want Him to."

After we prayed, Ginger went to sleep. Joe was happy about that. Ginger died during the night while Mom held her. Mom was quietly crying when I woke up. I was the first one to see Mom and Ginger in the morning. Mom said that Ginger's death would hurt all of us.

Joe was having a very hard time. Ginger usually slept on Joe's bed with him at night. Joe asked, "Why couldn't she have the surgery? Maybe she would still be alive today!" Joe said that he felt like he had lost his best friend.

Molly asked, "Will Ginger wake up tomorrow?"

Joe answered sharply, "Ginger is dead! She will never wake up!"

Dad and Mom were quiet. At the dinner table, Dad told Joe to talk about his feelings. Joe shouted, "Ginger shouldn't have been outside! She wouldn't be dead if she weren't by the gate. Tony shouldn't have let Ginger go through the gate."

Dad was calm. He put his hand on Joe's shoulder and reminded Joe how much Ginger liked to run. "She is hard to stop when she runs, and she loved to run! Tony was trying to stop her from running outside the gate. Tony feels bad that Ginger got out of the yard. He misses her too."

I wanted to cry. I did miss her. It startled me when Joe said to me, "Tony, I am so sorry for getting mad at you. I know it wasn't your fault."
We were all crying.
"Tomorrow," Dad finally aid, "we will bury Ginger in the back yard. Then we will have a memorial service for her."
Molly asked what a memorial service was. Dad said that we would all take turns saying what we liked the most about Ginger.
Joe, Molly, and I said we wanted Ginger to be buried by the shed. Molly said, "I want to put my wooden cross where we bury her."

When the time came, Joe helped Dad dig the whole to bury Ginger.

Joe started to cry again. Then I cried too. Joe said, "I think we will all miss Ginger."

***

The loss of a pet can be very painful emotionally. Our pets connect with us and are always with us, just as our immediate family is. They seem to be aware when we really need them. Dogs often protect us and are forgiving even when we are not having a very good day.

The whole family's grief may be very intense. As with any major loss, "it hurts so bad."

A ritual is important for children after the death of a pet. Give them choices about the burial or ritual. Children may want to choose where the pet will be buried. Any way they can participate in planning the ritual will help them to cope with the loss.

Encourage children and allow them to help whenever possible.

Chapter 3

Bullying

*And be ye kind one to another, tender hearted, forgiving
one another, even as God for Christ's sake
hath forgiven you.*
Ephesians 4:32

I am in the fourth grade. Our teacher, Mrs. Bates, is kind to everyone. She is even kind to Peter. We call him Stinky Pete. Every day when he comes to school, he stinks. His clothes are old. Sometimes he wears the same clothes all week.

Mrs. Bates sometimes give Stinky Pete a snack at recess. Usually, it is a peanut butter and jelly sandwich. He eats slowly, but he does seem hungry.

I try to talk to stinky Pete sometimes, but he doesn't talk much. He grunts. I know I hurt his feelings at least once.

The other kids used to laugh at him when he answered a question. His answers were always right, but now he looks the other way when Mrs. Bates asks questions about our work.

One day Mrs. Bates started to teach us about bullying. She said, "But wait!"

Everyone was so quiet that you could hear a pin drop.

Then Mrs. Bates asked, "How many of you have ever thrown darts or shot arrows?"

Several guys raised their hand, but no one said a word. She then asked how many were good at it. Only a few guys raised their hand. Then she asked, "What makes someone good at throwing darts or shooting arrows?"

Someone said, "Well, if you want to hit the target, you have to throw it hard."

"Very good," Mrs. Bates said. "Picture throwing an arrow or a dart at something. You try to hit what you are aiming at, right?"

Most of just said yes or uh-huh, and almost everyone nodded yes. Even Stinky Pete agreed.

"Now picture yourself throwing arrows or darts at *someone*."

It seemed like a long time before she said anything else.

"Now picture someone throwing arrows or darts at *you*. Then picture those arrows or darts as words."

A wound caused by an arrow or dart would hurt and probably leave a scar. Words like arrows would really hurt. Hurtful words might even be worse. Hurtful words sometimes don't heal and leave a lasting scar. A physical wound will heal, even if it leaves a scar. Hurtful words never fully heal.

Again, the room was so quiet that Mrs. Bates didn't have to tell anyone to quit talking.

Mrs. Bates continued, "Parents sometimes say harmful things to their children. They may say, 'You are getting fat,' 'You smell bad,' 'You aren't good at anything.' " She paused to let us think. "Bullying is like throwing arrows, and they hurt in a deep painful way."

Mrs. Bates said that our next writing project would be to write about bullying. "It could have been when an adult, sibling, or friend bullied us or when we bullied someone else. Words we said might be, 'We don't want you here,' 'You are fat,' 'You embarrass us, 'You are ugly,' or 'Even your mother probably doesn't love you because—'"

Mrs. Bates told our class that we needed to use the word "bully" or "bullying" in our writing project. We should tell of a time when either we were bullied or bullied someone else.

I wondered if ignoring someone who tried to be your friend would be like bullying. I thought about Stinky Pete. Once when he came towards me, I held my nose. I wanted him to see that I did that because I didn't want anyone to think that we were friends. I thought about the hurt look he had on his face. Now he doesn't even look at me. I wish I could take it all back. I know it hurt his feelings, but I didn't think it would *harm* him or leave a scar.

At home, Mom and Dad asked what we learned in school that day. I said our class learned about bullying. They wanted to know more. I told them that Mrs. Bates said throwing darts or arrows was a lot like bullying.

Molly Mae said, "I don't understand how shooting arrows is like bull-een."

"Mrs. Bates said that name calling or hurting other people's feeling is bullying," I said. "If you shoot an arrow at something, it can tear or ruin what you hit. If you tell someone they stink or are fat, that's like bullying because it will hurt them. She said that words can be very powerful and hurt others. Children can even bully their parents," I said.

Molly asked how we could bully our parents. I said that I thought it would be like trying to control them to get what you wanted. "If you begged and begged Mom about something you wanted, and she said no and then you went to Dad, and he said yes, that would be a little bit like bullying them. Mrs. Bates said that if you try to bully or control someone to get your way, that is one way you could be bullying them."

Dad said that he liked that definition. Molly said that she still didn't understand.

I told them that I didn't like to be around Cousin Tom. "Tom calls Jack names. When Jack is practicing the piano, Tom says that he isn't very good and calls him lousy. Aunt Betty tells Tom to stop it, but he doesn't. When Uncle Tim tells Tom to stop it, Tom stops."

Molly said, "So if someone tells me I am annoying, that is bull-een?"

Mom said, "Yes, Molly, and if you call someone names or make fun of them, that is also considered bullying."

CHAPTER 4

When a Sibling Faces Serious Illness

And pray for one another, that ye may be healed.
The effectual fervent prayer of a righteous man
availeth much.
James 5:15

One day in school, Mrs. Bates told us to write a story about our family. She said to write about our brothers and sisters. She told us that brothers and sisters are called "siblings," and we could write about one sibling, or more if we wanted to.

I thought about my sister, Molly Mae. She was so sick for days and days. After a week, Mom and Dad took her to the hospital. Molly did not come home that night. Mom didn't come home that night, either.

Mom stayed with Molly Mae in the hospital because Molly was so scared and had a lot of trouble breathing. The doctor told Mom and Dad that Molly could die. I burst into tears when Mom and Molly didn't even come home the next day.

The next morning, Dad told Joe and me that we needed to go to school. We didn't feel like going. I told Dad that I wasn't sick—"I'm just so tired."

Joe said that he had a bit of a sick stomach. Dad told us that it is normal not to feel good when someone in the family is sick and in the hospital. He said it is hard on all of us. Dad told us that Granddad and Grams would be here when we came home from school.

Grams had dinner cooked. She made macaroni and cheese, which is one of my favorites. Molly Mae loves it too. I missed Molly Mae so much. I missed her laugh.

Joe wasn't very talkative through dinner. He is usually funny and tells us about things that happened at school, and we all laugh.

The next day, Joe and I ran all the way home from school. I opened the front door and yelled for Mom and Molly. They were not home. Grams and Granddad were there. Grams had dinner ready for us again.

Dad came home late from the hospital. He seemed sad. He ate some dinner but said he wasn't hungry. He thanked Grams for dinner and then asked Granddad, Grams, Joe, and me to sit down in the front room so he could talk to us.

Dad started to cry. I had never seen Dad cry. He told us that the doctor said that if Molly didn't get better soon, she might die. He told us that she might need a breathing tube.

Joe asked, "What is a breathing tube?"

Dad explained that it was a tube that they put down a person's throat and then attach to a machine to help the person breathe.

Grams started to cry. Joe and I cried, too. I felt like I couldn't stop sobbing. It hurt my chest. Grams put her arms around Joe and me until we stopped crying.

The next day, I ran home again, but again Mom and Molly weren't there. Grams looked like she had been crying. She said that she had been praying to Jesus, asking Jesus to heal Molly Mae. She said that she had called the church and asked the prayer team to pray for Molly, too.

Grams told us about a scripture, James 5:13–15, that talks about healing. She said that she believed Jesus would heal Molly Mae.

The next day, Joe and I ran home together after school. Granddad and Gram's car and Dad's truck were in the driveway. Dad greeted us at the front door with a smile on his face. He told us that Molly Mae was much better and would probably come home tomorrow. We so happy that we all laughed.

Grams said, "Don't forget to stop and thank Jesus for healing Molly!"

I laughed again and told Grams that was something that Molly Mae would say!

Dad said that he was exhausted and wanted to go to bed early. Grams and Granddad also said that they were very tired and wanted to go home to get some rest. Joe told them he would fix something for both of us to eat. We again all laughed. I said that I just wanted a bowl of my favorite cereal.

Morning came, and Joe asked if he could stay home from school. He said that he didn't want to get out of bed. Dad told him that he could stay home one day, and he would have Grams check on him later. I asked if I could sleep in, too, and Dad said yes. He told us that he was going to go to work because keeping busy helped him keep his mind off things.

Grams came over. At noon, Granddad brought Mom and Molly home. She smiled when she saw Joe and me. She still had a cough that seemed to tire her, and she said that she was tired.

Grams and Mom hugged each other and cried. They started talking softly.

Granddad sat down in dad's recliner and opened his Bible. Soon he was snoring. We tried not to laugh—we didn't want to wake him up!

Grams told Mom that she would cook dinner before they went home. Mom said she would really appreciate that. She told Grams that she would like it if Grams made her special fried chicken. Grams smiled and said that she would.

After she put the dinner on the table, Dad walked into the house. He was smiling and hugged Mom and Grams. "Dinner smells so good!" he said. "I am very hungry."

Grams and Granddad left, and Dad asked Mom how she was doing. She said she was so happy to have the whole family home and together again. They started talking about how sick Molly Mae was and how difficult it had been for Joe and me to have the two of them gone. Dad said, "Now that Molly is better, we can all rest."

***

Tears can be very healing, just like laughter. They can be thought of as "healing waters." Try comforting those who cry and let them do it, rather than offering a Kleenex and encouraging them not to cry.

Exhaustion or feeling tired is one way the body reacts to stress. Crisis and loss cause stress, as do changes in the family unit. Take care of yourself by learning effective coping strategies so you can help your children throughout their lives.

CHAPTER 5

Getting Ready for the Move

*I will instruct thee and teach thee in the way that thou
shalt go; I will guide thee with mine eye.*
Psalm 32:8

Mom and Dad were talking about selling our house and moving. Dad was telling Mom that they needed to paint the living room and the kitchen. "I will stop at the paint store and get some paint," he said.

Mom said, "We should paint the walls white." Mom noticed I wasn't eating dinner and reminded me to eat, but I wasn't hungry.

Joe was very quiet. He wasn't talking about the funny things that happened at school, like he usually does. He kept sighing. Mom said, "Joe, you are sighing a lot. Sighing is a sign of grief. We will get through this big move together."

Molly asked, "What is grief?"

"It is the reaction we have," Mom explained, "when we have a loss or expect a loss, like when a pet or family member dies. It also happens when someone loses a job or a home. Joe is already missing his friends and feels upset about it."

Joe said, "I don't want to leave my friends!" He sounded irritated. "They have been my friends since I was in the first grade. Bill and Sam both told me that they will really miss me."

Molly started to cry. "I don't want to move, and I want my bedroom to be pink!"

Mom told Molly that we all would be getting new bedrooms in our new house.

Crying, Molly said, "I want my bedroom in this house to be pink!"

Mom said to Molly, "We will paint your new bedroom pink." Then she sat down on the floor. She told us to sit down next to her so we could talk about it.

"I do not want to talk about it!" Molly answered. But then she went to sit on Mom's lap.

"Do you know what the word 'cope' means?" Mom asked.

"No," the three of us answered together.

"Coping is what you do to help you get through hard things. There are probably a hundred ways to cope. Some people cry, some people pray, and some people like to write in a journal. Many people like to talk to someone about their feelings and what is bothering them."

"Is that like when I talk to Granddad when something really bothers me?" Joe asked.

"Yes," Mom said. "Some people don't like to talk to anyone when something really bothers them."

"Like when Uncle Erik says that he doesn't like to talk about his feelings?" I asked.

Mom said that Uncle Erik was very private about what bothers him. "He has always been like that. "Have you ever noticed," she went on to ask, "Granddad studying his Bible?"

"Yes," I said, "and he underlines a lot of the verses in his Bible. Sometimes he writes verses in his book and what the verses mean to him. Granddad calls it 'journaling.' I like to write things down in my journal, too.

"Granddad says when we journal, it helps us to look at things that just don't make sense!" I said. "Granddad says that he like to write down all his prayer requests, and later he goes back and reads them. He says that he sees where God has answered a lot of his prayers. and then he writes down the date!"

Mom asked us, "Can you now understand the word 'cope'?"

Joe and I laughed. "I guess so," Joe said. "I like to swing in the big swing when I am thinking about things."

"Is that a way to cope?" I asked.

Mom smiled. "It sure is!"

Mom and Joe started to laugh. Dad walked in the room as Molly and I started laughing too. "What is so funny?" Dad asked.

"Oh, we were just talking about ways to cope," I said, "and how there are many ways to do things."

Dad sat down with us. "I would like to hear more. How do each of you like to cope when you are going through hard things?"

We talked about ways we like to get through difficult things.

Dad said, "I am so happy to see that everyone seems to be 'coping' better than yesterday!"

Joe asked if we would be going to the same school. Dad said that we all would change schools and would be moving to a different town.

Joe pushed his chair back so fast from the table that it fell backwards. "I don't want to leave my friends! And I like my teacher!"

Mom chuckled a little. "Joe, you always like your teachers."

No one had finished dinner. Dad explained that the post office had offered him a better job that would pay more money. "You can still see your friends sometimes," he said to Joe. "You just won't be going to the same school."

"But we can't move away from Grams and Granddad's house," Joe said. "And we won't have the swing anymore!"

"What's this about not having a swing?" Dad said. "We will have our own swing. I will ask Granddad to help us build one, just like theirs."

CHAPTER 6

Coping Mechanisms and Strategies

But though he cause grief, yet will he have compassion
according to the multitude of his mercies. For he doth not
afflict willingly nor grieve the children of men.
Lamentations 3:32–33

Coping mechanisms are the strategies we use to help manage painful or difficult emotions during and after a stressful experience. They may be conscious or unconscious. The purpose of using them is to maintain a balanced equilibrium.

Defense mechanisms mostly happen at an unconscious level—people are unaware that they are using them. These can be learned behaviors.

Avoidance mechanisms are used to ignore the stress.

Attack mechanisms refers to fighting with someone rather than dealing with the real problem or issue.

Blaming is a mechanism that is a form of denial. Other maladaptive coping mechanisms to watch out for in your child include:

- escape or withdrawing from family and friends.
- depression for a long time after the loss.
- not wanting to live and even talking about ending their life.

Coping mechanisms are used to manage an external situation that is creating problems for your child. Following are fifteen coping strategies that you may find effective—keep trying until you find what works for your child in a given situation.

1. Let them cry it out. Cry with them.
2. Laugh together! Sometimes laughter helps and allows for release of tension after a loss.
3. Let them talk about their feelings or what is bothering them. Talk about yours too. It's normal to talk about feelings after any loss—101 times, if that's what they need. Don't discourage them talking, but give yourself a

break. If one parent gets tired of hearing the story, encourage your child to talk to other people as well. A support group is very helpful. Support groups can include being part of a team, such as participating in a sports, church or Sunday class, choir or band, or just being any place regularly where people meet and get to know one another.

4. Helping is therapeutic. In chapter 2, we saw Joe getting the box, holding Ginger, and helping with the burial and memorial service. Find a way to for your child to make connections.

5. Pray and study God's Word together.

6. Encourage your child to write out their feelings or experiences in a journal.

7. Family members can nurture one another, but accept support from others, too, as you go through grief or loss together. It's okay for the child to nurture or support an adult, but be careful that the child does not become the parent.

8. Returning to school or work is healthy. It is a way to return to normalcy. But don't misinterpret returning to work or school as the person "coping well"—it coping strategies are more than just keeping busy.

9. Take care of yourself and encourage your child to do the same. That means adequate sleep and rest, drinking plenty of water, and eating nutritious food, even if it is frequent small meals, and increasing protein in your diet.

10.   Try to keep a normal routine as much as possible. Try not to move or change schools, if you can—but if the loss is a parent or significant caregiver, it may not be possible to stay in the same house or return to same school.

11. Teach children to be dependent. Everyone needs to know how to cook, so teaching a child at an early age to cook and clean has many benefits. Being present for to your child in doing tasks is a way to be mutually supportive. These lifelong skills teach independence and help children value themselves by accomplishing something that they can enjoy and take pride in, maybe even in the eyes of their friends.

12.   Encourage play!

13.   Keep children active. In addition to support groups as mentioned in number 3, many children like to draw, color, and paint as a way to show expression.

14. Encourage friendships. Those support groups such as team sports and Sunday School give children the opportunity to grow up together with like minds and become true friends.

15.   If children like music, books, and movies, support them in finding music and stories that help them deal with loss. For younger children, *Charlotte's*

Web is a gentle way of showing loss and the emotions that go with it. You can look up a list of books and movies online.

A last note on finances. If money is an issue in your family, and someone asks how they can help, let them! Tell them that your child likes certain books, movies, art supplies, sports equipment, or whatever. If your child is age nine or older and would like to play a musical instrument, talk with your the school or music teacher. They may have good options.

People may not always know what to say but really want to help. Letting people in is a way to include them as part of your own support group.

CHAPTER 7

Cognitive and Psychosocial Development

When I was a child, I spake as a child, I understood as a child,
I thought as a child: but [then] I became a man.
1 Corinthians 13:11 (KJV)

A child must be told that the person is dead. Children are concrete in their thinking, so being direct is the best way to tell them. Don't use the words such as "deceased," "passed on," "are on a long journey," or "went to heaven to be with Jesus." Don't try to prepare children—or anyone else, for that matter. Say, "Grandpa is dead. He died this morning." Don't start off by saying, "I have very bad news for you. Please stop what you are doing and come and talk with me." Try to take your child or children to a safe, warm place to talk with them.

Children need to grieve and process their loss through every developmental stage in their life. Remember, no matter how old children may be, they just have experienced the worst tragedy in their young lives if a parent, grandparent, or close caregiver has died.

It may be helpful for you to understand the cognitive and psychosocial developmental stages, based on Piagetian and Eriksonian psychology, to help children process loss or major events in their lives.

Birth to age 2

Piagetian cognitive stage
Sensorimotor stage

- views life through the senses (touch, smell, taste, sight, hearing)
- perceives that significant others (parents or caregivers) or things come and go
- learns through senses and movement

Eriksonian psychosocial stage
Trust versus mistrust: attachment to significant person
Trust develops when loved one is again present
Reactions to loss: general distress; cries; fitful sleep
Child's concept of death: no concept of death but reacts to loss

Helpful approaches: consistent nurturing person

Ages 2-7
Piagetian cognitive stage
Preoperational stage
Cannot reason beyond what they see, hear, or experience

Eriksonian stages of psychosocial development

Ages 1–3
-Autonomy versus shame and doubt
-Sense of dependence and self-control
(3–5)
*Initiative versus guilt
*Ability to initiate activities and see them though
-Reaction to loss
(2–5)
-Confusion, fear, nightmares
-Understands profound event has occurred
-May seem unaffected by loss
-May react to others' emotions
*Child's concept of death
-Death is temporary and reversible
-Death is seen as a departure or separation
*Helpful approaches
-Reassurance
-Drawing
-Funeral ritual
-Play
(5)
+Ericksonian stages of psychosocial development
-Compare his abilities with other children
*Reaction to loss
-Understanding death or loss is limited
(5–8)
-Wants to understand death in concrete manner
-Denial, anger, fear, sadness
-Thinks it won't happen to them

(7–11)

+Piagetian cognitive stage of development

-Period of informal operations

-Thought becomes logical

-Can consider points of view other than his own

+Eriksonian stages of psychosocial development

(5–12)

-Industry versus inferiority

-Successful teaching of self against peers leads to feelings of industry

*Reactions to loss

(5–8)

-General distress and confusion

-May act as though nothing has happened

(8–12)

-May want to conform with peers

*Child's concept of death

-Death is irreversible but not necessarily inevitable

-Death may be personified and viewed as destructive

-Explanations for death are naturalistic and physiological

*Helpful approaches

-Simple honesty

-Answer questions simply

-Dead is dead

-Physical outlets

-Play, color, draw, reading, sculpting

+Funeral ritual, including helping with the planning of the funeral.

-Reassurance about the future

-Talking about feelings

-Keeping a journal

(12–15)

*Piagetian cognitive stage of development

-Period of formal operations characterized by adaptability and flexibility

*Eriksonian stages of psychosocial development

-Identity versus role confusion

*Reactions to loss

-Shock, anxiety, distress, anger, denial, depression, despair

-Fewer coping mechanisms than adults have

-Façade of coping: "It's okay" when it's not okay
-Finality of death is understood
Phobic behaviors
Morbid curiosity
*Child's concept of death
-Death is irreversible, universal, and inevitable
-Death is still seen as a personal but event distant
-Explanations for death are physiological and theological
*Helpful approaches
-Discussing feelings
-Peer support groups
-Consistent environment

REFERENCES

Bates, M. and Keirsey, D. *Please Understand Me*. Delmar: Prometheus Nemesis Book Company, 1984.

Collins, G. *How to Be a People Helper*. Ventura: Regal Books, 1975.

Darley, G. M., Glucksberg, S., and Kinchla, R.A. *Psychology,* 5th ed. New Jersey: Prentice Hall, 1991.

Deits, B. *Life after Loss*. Tucson: Fisher Books, 1988.

Hemfelt, R., and Warren, P. *Kids Who Carry Our Pain*. Nashville: Thomas Nelson, 1990.

Martin, V. *The Morning after Mourning*. Bloomington, IN.: WestBow Press, 2020.

Printed in the United States
by Baker & Taylor Publisher Services